ONE HUNDRED

Muddy Paws
For Thought

ONE HUNDRED

Muddy Paws
For Thought

BY
Simon Whaley

ILLUSTRATIONS BY
Jilly Wilkinson

Hodder & Stoughton
LONDON SYDNEY AUCKLAND

British Library Cataloguing in Publication Data
A record for this book is available from
the British Library

ISBN 0 340 86347 1

Typeset in Baskerville by Avon DataSet Ltd,
Bidford-on-Avon, Warwickshire

Printed and bound in Great Britain by
Bookmarque Ltd, Croydon, Surrey

The paper and board used in this paperback are natural
recyclable products made from wood grown in sustainable
forests. The manufacturing processes conform to the
environmental regulations of the country of origin.

Hodder & Stoughton
A Division of Hodder Headline Ltd
338 Euston Road
London NW1 3BH
www.madaboutbooks.com

To Mum, Dad, Claire and Grandma
(who've all seen active duty with a dog and a
towel, and tried to bring the two together)

Contents

Canine Cosmetics

Humans wear make-up. Your make-up is mud. Wear yours with pride.

Humans wear make-up for special occasions – such as when they have a dinner party and invite all their best friends round to your home. Don't be left out. Always try to wear your make-up for their special occasions too.

Humans wear perfume in strategic places, such as behind their ears or on their wrists. It doesn't matter where you wear your perfume, just as long as the cause of the smell remains matted in your fur for several days.

Never let a human's facial expression and the holding of their nose concern you. Remember that it is you who has the far superior sense of smell, and therefore only you can really appreciate the full bouquet of your acquired aroma.

Women wear mudpacks to help keep their skin young, and look beautiful. Show your human how beautiful you can look with a muddy face too.

Car and Kitchen Capers

Responsible humans like to know where you are at all times. Be considerate and tell them where you've been, by leaving a trail of muddy footprints across all floor surfaces.

As you get older, you may find it more difficult to jump in and out of the rear of the car, when your human takes you out for exercise. Encourage them to buy a ramp that will let you climb gently in and out. These are often advertised in those catalogues that come free with the Sunday newspapers. Carefully drop the catalogue into their lap when they are asleep. If your human doesn't take the hint, next time you get into the car, ensure your claws are fully extended as you try and grip their colour-coded bumper, and clamber in.

Canine service broadcasts can be seen throughout the day on your human's TV. Watch how the dog trots across the kitchen floor with muddy feet, and then see how the human cleans it all up. At the end of the broadcast, notice how the dog wags its tail and the human gives it a loving pat on the head. Try to get your human to emulate this. Keep putting dirty footprints on the kitchen floor until your human gets in the habit of cleaning it up, and then patting you lovingly on the head.

Repetition of the kitchen footprint pattern can also demonstrate your willingness to become a canine actor. If your humans don't understand the message, touch the screen with one of your paws when the canine service broadcast in question comes on, and bark loudly. (Even better if you can touch the screen with the dirtiest of your paws.)

Many household cleaning products claim to bring the aroma of the fresh outdoors, indoors. Forget the aroma – why not just bring the whole lot in!

Having got back in the car to come home, wait until your human has shut all the car doors, put on their seat belt and started the engine, before shaking any excess moisture off your coat.

Clever humans will buy cars with leather upholstery, as this is easier to wipe clean. Cars with fabric upholstery stain easily and become a memory bank of all your previous exciting walks. Enjoy adding to this collection.

In winter when it's wet and windy, your humans may wash your feet and dry them with a towel every time you come in from the garden (having done some 'business'). Humans enjoy spending this extra time with you. Bond better with your human by drinking lots more water and doing lots more 'business'. (Just don't drink the

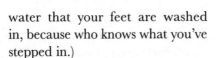

water that your feet are washed in, because who knows what you've stepped in.)

Some humans prefer their dogs to sit in the rear of the car behind a dog guard or in a safety cage. Other humans buy harnesses to secure you to the seat belts, allowing you to have the back seats to yourself. Push your human for this second option. Back-seat passengers are chauffeur-driven, whereas dogs in the back of hatchbacks and estates are taken places. This is a subtle but important difference. Be chauffeured, not taken.

Humans collect souvenirs when on holiday, so why don't you take your favourite stick or pebble home with you? Always growl and snarl though, if your human tries to take it out of the car to throw it away. Where you sit in the car should always be filled with happy holiday mementos for years to come. Ignore your human's mutterings about deteriorating fuel consumption due to the extra weight.

Canine Catalogues

A new collar should always be baptised as soon as it starts raining. Make sure it is a different colour to what it was when your human first put it on you. You have ten minutes in which to achieve this. Getting it to the right colour and stickiness means that no one will want to grab hold of it.

Dissuade your owner from buying you a personalised pet jacket. Let's face it, after you've been through all fourteen swamps on your usual Sunday afternoon stroll, no one's going to be able to read the name on your jacket anyway, are they?

S ave your human some money. Don't let them buy those special dog beds with fake paw

prints dotted all over them, when you can do it yourself on the sofa!

Catalogues sell those all-in-one dog drying bags, designed to completely envelope you (and your dirt), up to your neck. Humans like them because they keep the car clean on your journey home. Use your snotty nose to dirty the rear windscreen instead.

Fluorescent leads are very safe when out walking in the dark. Make it even safer by walking on the verge and getting your human to walk on the outside of you (in the road).

It's possible to get canine sunglasses, so you and your human can 'chill out' together and try to look alluring to the opposite sex. Condition your human into letting you wear them on a regular basis to get used to them. Sunglasses create the perfect excuse – you won't be able to see the mess you're getting yourself into.

Your human can purchase a special mat to put by their

door, designed to collect all the dirt from your feet as you trot over it. Why not show your human how fit you are by jumping straight over it instead?

It could be argued that being thoroughly cleaned by your human occasionally can make getting dirty next time that bit more enjoyable. Let your human win once in a while and use all the cleaning products they've bought for you. At least *you* know you won't be clean for long.

The more expensive anti-tangle dog shampoo is now available to help keep your fur in pristine condition. Insist that your human buys it and uses it on you once in a while. Why? Because you're worth it!

After you've been washed with your special doggy shampoo in the bath, don't let your human waste electricity by drying you with the hairdryer. Apart from it being dangerous to use electricity so close to water, it's far easier for you to rub yourself dry on your human's duvet instead.

The Great Outdoors

It's only since humans have domesticated dogs that you've had to be clean. Go ancestral. Get dirty!

If your human takes you somewhere new for a walk, it is better

to let them lead the way. If you get lost, it will be their fault, and not yours.

Humans are sometimes awarded the 'Freedom of the City', which allows them to wander unhindered through the streets. If you are awarded the 'Freedom of the Country' try not to abuse your freedom. You will know if you have because your human will not let you off your lead.

There will come a time when your human will need to clean you up. Enjoy the chase, but give them hope by letting them catch you briefly before you slip away again. It's a really good way to transfer some of your dirt onto their clothes.

When it's time to go out for a walk again, fetch your human's soil-caked Wellington boots and place them in their lap as

a reminder. Your human will be so pleased that they didn't waste their time by cleaning their boots, only to get them dirty again.

L earn to understand geology. A place with a high rock content has very little dirt or living matter. Any pools of water will therefore be relatively clean. Avoid these at all costs as clean water just defeats the whole exercise of a trip to the countryside.

A good day's rambling is always best finished off in a beautiful country pub. If you are especially dirty, you may find yourself and your human banished to the beer garden, but all is not lost. With some excessive shaking, and a good ten minutes of scratching your ear with a hind leg and making lots of ecstatic moaning noises, you should have the whole beer garden to yourselves.

Some dogs have to work in the outdoors for their living. Large country estates sometimes hold pheasant shoots where owners kill birds and then send in their dogs to retrieve the kill. These dogs belong to humans who are highly trained and can shoot straight. Can your human shoot straight? If your human cannot park the car within the white lines at a car park, don't take them anywhere near a pheasant shoot. Not if you value your life.

On those wet, windy, wintry walks when you're as dirty and as slimy as you can get, don't slip and slide frenetically as you try to clamber over a stile. Let your human sweep you up into their arms and gently carry you over, while you watch the remnants of that cow pat transfer from your coat to theirs.

Dog-friendly stiles are a mis-nomer. You either have to be the size of a mouse to squeeze through the hole provided, or have a human intelligent enough to work out how to operate it. Forget the hassle; just get your human to lift you over.

Kissing gates – the backwards and forwards movements can be very confusing. Let your human show you how it works and then feign stupidity, making out that you don't understand. If they'll carry you over the stiles, they can carry you through the kissing gates as well.

Never let your human carry you across a farm gate alone. The height of these means it's better to have two humans – one either side of the gate. One to pick you up and lift you across the gate, while the other can take you and gently put you back down on the ground on the other side. If your human insists on doing this alone, ask them to carry out a risk assessment first, pointing out that six months off work with a bad back may not qualify for payment under your pet insurance.

Bridges with wooden slats can be difficult to cross. Humans have only two legs to worry about where to put them in order to miss the space in between, whereas you have twice the confusion to contend with. You've got two choices. Go through the stream that the slatted bridge crosses, or get your human to carry you.

Duckboards are wooden paths designed to help keep humans out of particularly boggy patches of ground. They can be covered with chicken wire to prevent your human from slipping. Catching your nails in the chicken wire can be painful, so avoid duckboards at all costs. Go through the bog instead, or jump into your human's arms.

Take care with all this carrying that your humans are doing. You don't want to end up getting carried for the whole walk, do you? How else will you get dirty?

Whistle in the Wind

Your human will try to control you, even though you may have been awarded 'Freedom of the Country', by whistling their commands at you. Remember that thick bracken, grass or bushy undergrowth inhibits a human's whistle from penetrating your ears so find some and bury yourself in it as soon as you can.

When your human gets frustrated at your lack of response (you'll know this when the whistle becomes very high-pitched) always raise your head above the undergrowth with a facial expression that says, 'Oh! You're trying to call me!' while desperately looking for any other dog in the vicinity.

Watch and learn from the TV programme *One Man and His Dog*. It will be a long time before your human reaches that that level of skill (if at all), so you'll have to anticipate what you think your human wants you to do, rather than what they are actually whistling at you to do. Remember, if you fail to anticipate what they want you to do, it's not your fault; it's theirs for not making their instructions clear in the first place.

Learn to distinguish between the whistle commands 'Don't go near that filthy water' and 'Go and wash yourself off'. One uses a 'B flat' while the other uses a 'B sharp' and humans forget that a change in wind direction can alter the pitch of a whistled command.

S ome humans buy little 'clickers' to try and train you when you're outside. They only buy these because they themselves can't whistle or are just too lazy to try and learn. Well, if they can't be bothered to learn to whistle why should you bother to listen to clicks?

Rolling Rules

Always sit in a muddy puddle. When your human shouts angrily at you, wag your tail with excitement. This swishing movement has three positive effects:

- It means more of your tail gets bathed in the aromatic water.
- More of the most pungent particles that have sunk to the bottom of the puddle are stirred up and captured in your tail, as lovely, thick, sticky globules.
- These globules can then be thrown at your human's face with a quick flick, when they get close enough to you.

Learn Mother Nature's guide to pongability. The easier and longer that it sticks to your fur, the whiffier the pong will be. Here's the definitive list, starting with the least sticky (it will just drop off your coat of its own accord) to the stickiest (which will require six months of regular hosing down before it starts to shift).

- Rabbit dung
- Sheep dung
- Pigeon dung
- Fox dung
- Your own dung
- Another dog's dung
- Goose dung
- Horse dung
- Cow dung (fresh, of course)

There are also several tried and tested techniques for getting dirty. These include:

The Top to Toe

This involves lying down on your stomach in a suitable substance, and then rolling over onto your preferred side. Continue over on to your back and then follow through on to your other side. Return to your feet, shake off excess material, and then repeat if required. This gives an all-round coverage and strong aroma.

The Phantom of the Opera

This is excellent for fooling your human and giving your coat time to dry out. Lie down on one side with your face in the mud/mess. Using your back legs push away so that your whole body rotates

48

around your eye. This really grinds the dirt into the side of your head. If you stand up, only one side of your face will be dirty, while the other remains clear. Always keep your human to the clean side of you, preventing them from seeing the dirty side for as long as possible.

The Footballer's Dive

Grass stains are great and can take days to fade. Run like the clappers and then dive, turning your face so that you get a green grass streak from your eyebrow to the back of your head. Repeat on the other side of your face for symmetry.

The Hip and Thigh Blotch

This is similar to the Phantom of the Opera, and works well if used in conjunction with it, rather than instead of it. Lie on the ground with your hip in the mess of your choice. Using your front paws this time, push yourself around in a circular direction to grind the dirt in. This may create dirt streaks on your shoulder blades too.

The Belly Plop

This works best with wet material, preferably of at least two inches deep. Find your material and stand over it. First sit down, and then stretch out your front legs so you gradually lower yourself into the substance. Wait ten seconds before standing up. Should too much liquid drip off, repeat the process.

The Paint Brush

Dogs with bushy tails can 'dip' them in stagnant ponds, preferably ones close to home. Carry your tail curled under your body between your back legs to hide it from your human. When you get back home, stand with your back to the wall and wag your tail eagerly to show the rest of the family what a good time you've had on your walk. This works best on light-coloured walls and delicate wallpapers.

The Iron Mask

Close your eyes, stick your head in any murky water and then bring it back out. Blow through your nostrils to expel any excess murky water and slowly open your eyes. While your new mask is drip-drying, go and find some new human friends. You know the type – those who are oblivious to you because they're lying in the sun soaking up the rays. Lean over their faces and watch with delight as a remaining drop of murky substance falls from your nostril onto their cheek. Your own human likes to make friends with other humans this way.

The Bomb

Probably one of the best. Find the largest pond that you can, take the longest run up, leap and spread all your legs as wide as you can. It makes one heck of a splash but it really covers you. You'll find pond life under your armpits for weeks to come.

Seaside Seduction

When humans return home from a day at the beach, they will always find some sand in between their toes, in their hair and their coat pockets. Always follow the example that your family set you. In fact, why not make it a competition to see who can smuggle the most sand back home without any of the others realising?

You can always tell how pungent a rock pool is by the number of flies circulating above it.

Always cross an estuary mudflat to get to the tidal water so you can wash off the mud. Now look back at your human as they try to think how they're going to get you back on dry land, without you going through the mud again. Occasionally they will encourage you to walk along the estuary edge, while they desperately seek somewhere clean and dry for you to get out. Enjoy all your time in the water while you can. See how long they spend doing this, before they realise the only way to get you out is for them to come and get you, or to just let you get muddy again.

A freshly dirtied dog will go places – mainly because humans will get out of your way to avoid their bodies coming in contact with your recently contaminated coat. This works really well on a Bank Holiday Monday at the coast.

Beach bingo is a game that involves being the fastest to roll in a dead fish, a dead crab, rotting seaweed and a dead seagull. The winner is often rewarded with a swim in the sea.

There are always some substances that should be avoided at all times. Beaches with tar and oil on them may look fun, but after your human has spent all evening cutting it out of your fur, do you really want the bald Dalmatian look?

Tracking Tricks and Seasonal Scents

I f you fancy a longer walk than usual, pretend that you've got the scent of something big and dash off into the undergrowth. Ignore any commands that your human may shout, and they'll be forced to follow you.

B etter still, follow your nose when your human is attached to you by your lead. That way you'll discover if your human enjoys getting dirty too! You may even be able to compare scents with each other afterwards.

Having done this to your human, when you return to the car park that's packed with other humans, always walk around the muddy puddles. That way the other humans will think that you're such a nice dog trying hard to keep clean, and it's your human that insists on making you dirty.

Tracking provides the perfect excuse for getting dirty. After all, you've got no control over which way the scent leads, or what it leads through, have you?

Sometimes a scent can be lost in water. Avoid any embarrassment by picking up any other scent on the opposite side of the bank and follow that one instead.

Mother Nature brings a variety of aromas and substances throughout the year. Here's a seasonal guide to the best of the outdoors:

Winter

Holly berries and rosehips, either natural or already processed by the birds. Sticky and gooey, they have amazing fur-clumping qualities. Frozen cobwebs quickly thaw in your fur and this extra moisture always helps other dead matter to stick to your fur.

Spring

The season of new life. Toad- and frogspawn get particularly pungent if allowed to dry in your coat. Fresh grass cuttings are great because spring grass tends to be wetter than its summer counterpart. And for a slightly different aroma, why not try flower pollen, especially from fallen catkins, or daisies and buttercups? Dandelion clocks can be fun to spread around the house, but care should always be taken

with seeds as they can get into your skin, resulting in a trip to the vet.

Summer

Oh, the joys of stagnant pond water, undisturbed by flowing waters since the rain stopped falling in May, and the collection of rotten

fruit lying under trees, half-eaten by insects, and the occasional dead fish for that real month-long aroma that hangs around no matter how many times you are bathed in dog shampoo!

Autumn

A time of natural death and therefore greater stickiness. The ground is littered with squashed wild blackberries, rotting dank

leaves, fragile fungi and wild mush-
rooms. All just lying there on the
floor. Invitingly easy. (Avoid horse
chestnut trees though. Conker cases
are very prickly!)

Park Strife

Fed up with going to the same old place every day for your walk? Get your own back by always rolling in some dirt just before you get back to the car. Make sure though that you've already passed any washing facilities such as streams or ponds. If you are taken back to a pond to be washed off, roll again in the dirt. Are you taken back to the pond one more time? Well then, roll one more time. See who gives up first. Nine out of ten dogs said their humans soon gave in.

Never carry out any solid-type 'business' when being taken for a walk in playing fields or where children might play, particularly if your human doesn't use a poop-a-scoop. Your 'business' can be dangerous to children's health. Wait until you've got back home and are in the lounge. Your human will certainly learn to poop-a-scoop at home.

Some local authorities provide cardboard poop-a-scoops in recreation areas, which can become soft and disintegrate when wet. Always carry out your business when it's raining, or in long wet grass, and watch your human dash towards the poop-a-scoop bins as quickly as possible. Clearly the further away from the bins you do your 'business', the harder your human has to run to prevent disintegration.

Be proud of your human. Show the world how responsible your human is, by doing some 'business' in front of as many people as possible, when you're out. Watch with pride as your human poop-a-scoops it up and puts it in their pocket or bag until they find a dog bin or get home.

Sometimes it's nice to go out for a walk with your human and find that it's just you two in the park, and you've got the whole place to yourselves. This is usually because it's pouring with rain.

The great outdoors is all about finding the right stick. A good stick will remain stable in your jaws when you run up behind people and hit them in the back of the legs with it.

If there are lots of people about and you don't think you'll be able to remember which ones you've hit on the back of the legs with your stick, find a really muddy one. This will leave a good mark on the human's clothes for all to see.

Some humans make playing this game of 'tag' difficult by running away from you. See how many strangers you can get to join in as you play this game. If there are a lot of strangers you may need to make yourself even muddier and wetter, to really make your mark on everyone.

Gardener's Whirled

Try to help out your human with any gardening chores, such as digging holes in the soil to plant seeds in. About three feet deep is usually deep enough.

Compost heaps are much more productive if they are regularly turned to allow air into the material. Why not have a really good roll to stir it up and invigorate it?

Fishponds should be cleaned of excess weeds on a regular basis. Climbing in and stirring things up will help you determine how much weed there is in the first place.

Watering a garden is an important part of gardening. Help out with your own direct watering method wherever you can. (Best leave the hanging baskets to the humans though.)

Weeding keeps a garden nice and tidy. A weed is merely a plant in the wrong place. If you don't like where a plant is, then dig it out. You'll know it was a weed when your human plants it somewhere else in the garden.

Garden birds like to scavenge newly planted seedbeds looking for food. Protect your human's

vegetable patch by frightening them away. Really stamp your feet about the vegetable patch to show birds how angry you are.

Beware of hedgehogs. Always brootle about in a pile of leaves thoroughly before having a good roll in them. Rolling on a hedgehog is worse than having a booster jab at the vet's. About a hundred times worse!

Squirrels bury food in the garden for winter. Why don't you try the same?

Foxes are becoming urban creatures scavenging for food. Avoid the blame when you accident-ally knock over your human's dust-bin, by barking ferociously and looking at the top of the fence expectantly. The noise will attract your human who will think that you've frightened a fox away. They may even praise you for it.

Wait until you have your human's undivided atten-

tion when you want to show them the exciting creature that you've just found in the back garden. Drop it into their knickers while they're sitting on the toilet.

Why Is It?

Why is it that humans always want you to be clean, but they're the ones who take you out for a walk in that dirty countryside?

Why is it always the dog out for a walk that finds the dead body on those police TV programmes?

Why is it that when you're up to your armpits in heavenly mud, your human thinks that you'll come running back to them for one measly dog biscuit?

Why is it called a 'lead' when it's the human who takes a dog out for a walk, yet they are never the ones to do any leading?

Why is it the sandiest beaches that have dog bans?

Why is it that the first signs of dog old age are grey or white hairs around the eyes, when their faces are so often covered in brown mud?

Why is it that when dogs go out they just step outside, but when humans go out they have to put on:

- Suitable shoes with the appropriate socks
- A base layer that allows body moisture to escape
- A thermal layer to keep the torso warm
- An outer waterproof layer in case it rains
- A hat
- A scarf
- Some gloves
- Waterproof trousers
- Sunglasses (even if it isn't sunny)

Why is it that humans love the countryside except when it's in their living-rooms?

Why is it that no one has bred a dog with Gore-Tex™ fur? One shake (somewhere appropriate of course) and all would be clean.

Why is it that a human's poor sense of smell can only detect the 'nice' smells and label them as 'gut-wrenching' awful ones?

W hy is it that when a human shouts, 'Don't go anywhere near that water!' one look from the dog enables them to read their human's mind and then do the exact opposite?

W hy is it that after the average dog's lifespan of fifteen years, during which time humans will have:

- taken them on 10,956 walks;
- bathed them 780 times;
- fed them 5,478 meals;
- wiped mud off the walls at least 10,956 times;

- disinfected the kitchen floor 43,824 times;

. . . they still love their dogs?